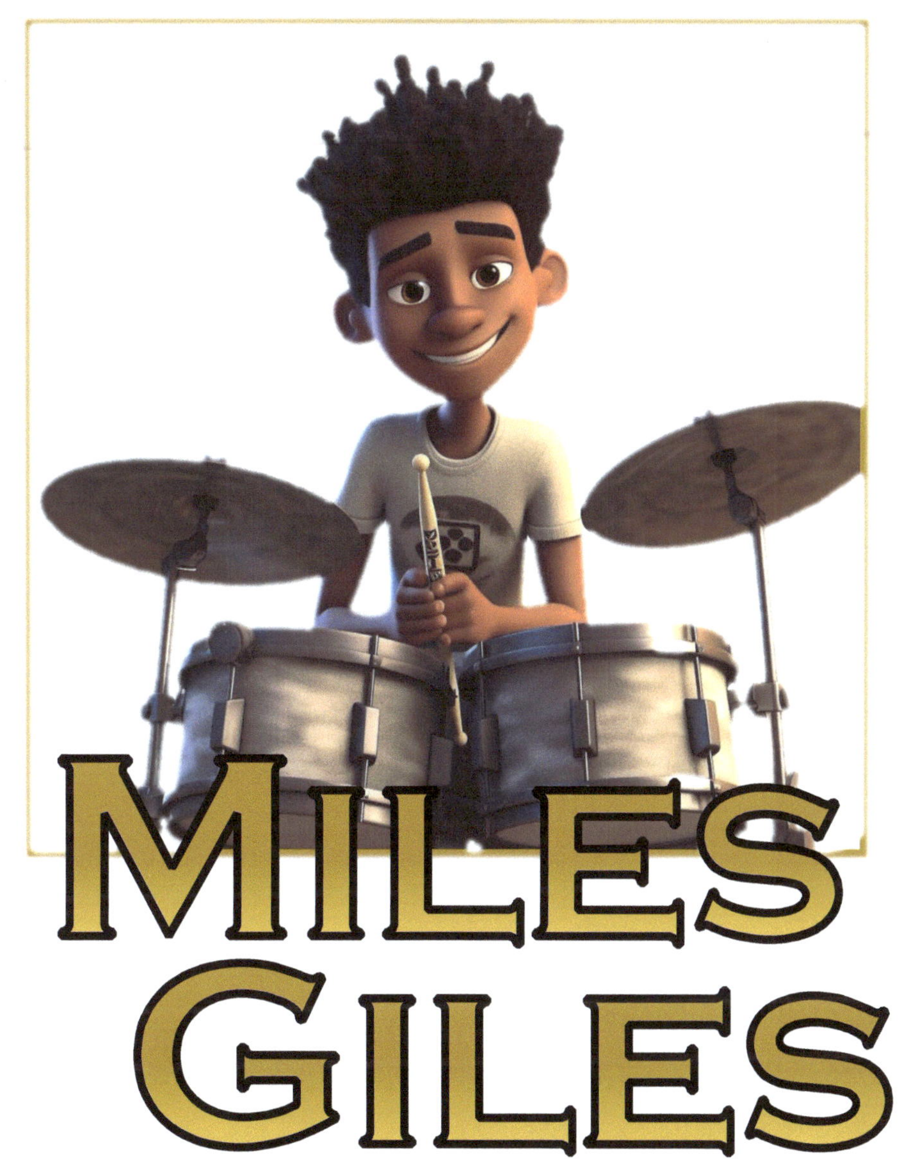

MILES GILES

THE RHYTHM IN HIS HEART

T. BENTON-PARKER

Mission: To Proclaim Transformation and Truth

Publisher: Transformed Publishing, Cocoa, FL

Website: www.transformedpublishing.com

Email: transformedpublishing@gmail.com

ISBN: 978-1-953241-46-7

DEDICATION

To my brother, David Cooper &

with love to Victor Giles 10/10/2020

Miles Giles

10-months

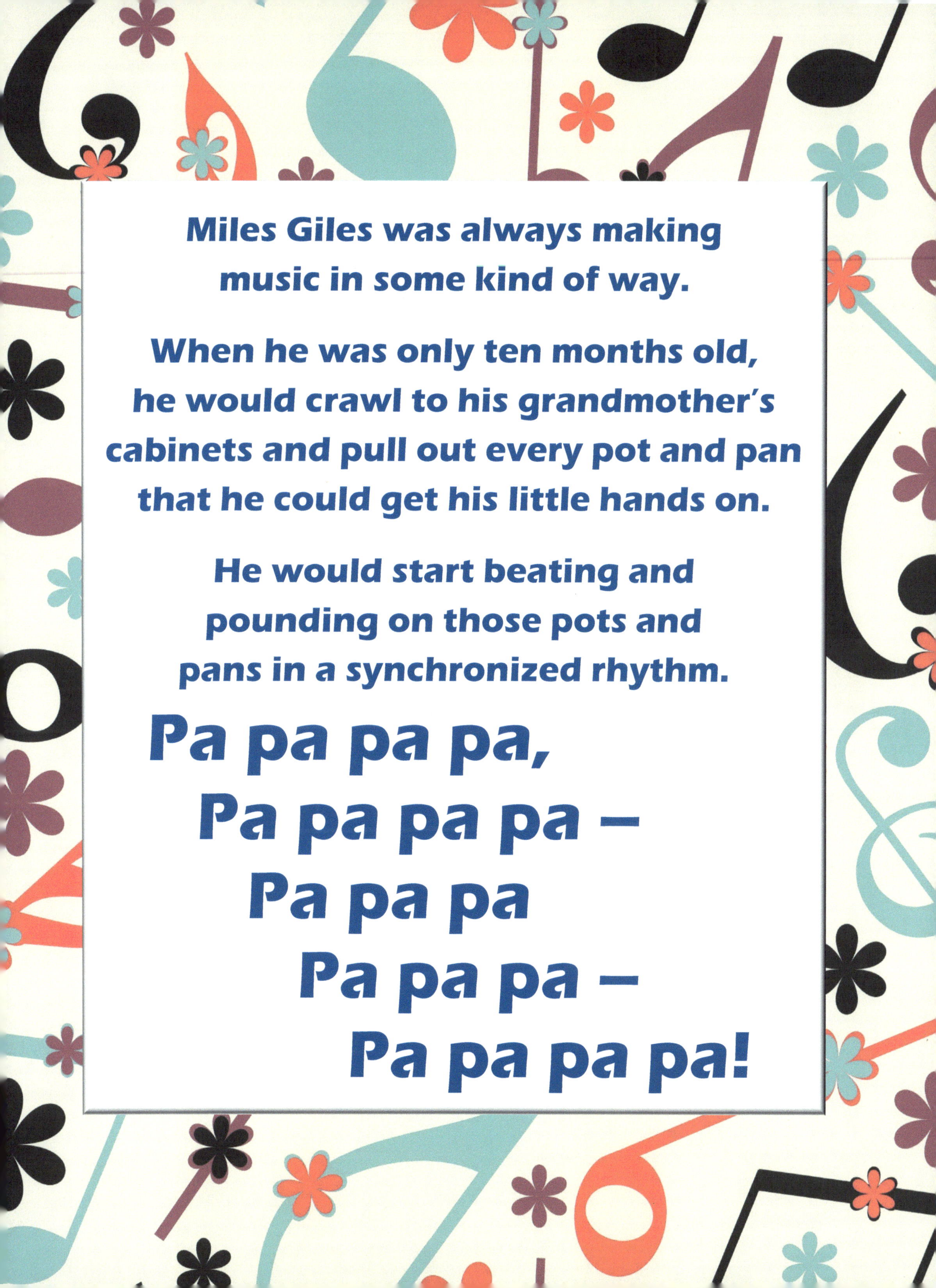

Miles Giles was always making music in some kind of way.

When he was only ten months old, he would crawl to his grandmother's cabinets and pull out every pot and pan that he could get his little hands on.

He would start beating and pounding on those pots and pans in a synchronized rhythm.

Pa pa pa pa,
Pa pa pa pa –
Pa pa pa
Pa pa pa –
Pa pa pa pa!

But Grandma never stopped him or said a word.

But she would say to him, "My little musical Miles – you're going to be a musician some day!" And she would give him the biggest smile.

It was Thanksgiving Day and the family was watching the famous Macy's Day Parade.

As the band marched across the TV screen, so did Miles. He grabbed the nutcracker that was sitting on Mama's fancy new table and began to beat the melody that he heard.

Pa pa pa pa,
Pa pa pa pa –
Pa pa pa
Pa pa pa –
Pa pa pa pa!

"Oh, no!" shouted Mama, "Not my new table!"

But it was too late! Miles had hundreds
of little dents all on his mother's new
wooden table. Mama was not pleased.

But, Grandma gave him the biggest smile
and said, "My musical Miles is getting
better every day. You know,
he's going to be a musician some day!"

Miles Giles

5 years old

When Miles Giles was five years old,
his mom and dad bought him his own
little drum set. He would spend hours
and hours entertaining himself.

You could hear him play the beats
that he heard in his head.

When Miles started elementary school
his love for the melodic sound of
synchronized rhythms got him in trouble.

He would take the end of his pencil and beat
the rhythms he imagined on the desk.

Pa pa pa pa,

Pa pa pa pa –

Pa pa pa

Pa pa pa –

Pa pa pa pa!

The class altogether would say,

"sSSShhhhhh!"

The teacher would give him the stare.

When he stopped, she would always say, "Miles Giles, I know some day you're probably going to be a famous musician, but for today, you can't distract the class."

When Miles Giles was in sixth grade, his music teacher chose him to play the bongos for the fall festival concert.

She told him to find the rhythm in his heart. So, he practiced and practiced.

He memorized every pattern.

Pa pa pa pa,
Pa pa pa pa –
Pa pa pa
Pa pa pa –
Pa pa pa pa!

The fall festival was here and Miles Giles was ready. The students loved it! Grandma was so proud sitting out there amongst the crowd. She yelled out, "That's my Miles! He's going to be a famous musician some day!"

When Miles Giles entered high school,
he joined the school marching band.

You could hear those drums as the
band marched across the field.
Grandma never missed a performance.

"There goes my Miles!" Grandma said excitedly.

The people in the stadium loved the band.
They loved the drum section even more!
You could hear Miles Giles playing . . .

Pa pa pa pa,
Pa pa pa pa –
Pa pa pa
Pa pa pa –
Pa pa pa pa!

When Miles Giles was in college,
he was chosen for the famous
Marching 100 Band in Tallahassee, Florida.

He could feel the rhythm of all of the
other instruments filling the air
as they all played in unison.

Pa pa pa pa,
Rat ta tat tat,
Toot, toot, toot, toot
Cling, cling, cling

The fans in the audience loved it!

The crowd grew wild for Miles Giles . . .
And Grandma cheered as he played on . . .

His grandma was right!
His teacher was even right!
His music teacher was right, too!
Miles Giles did grow up to be a famous
musician, like Ringo Starr, Ginger Baker,
Alex Van Halen, Travis Barker, and more.

He loved what he did and appreciated
the encouragement his grandma
always gave him.

Before he started every set,
he would say to himself,
*This one is for my grandma, she will
forever be the drumbeat of my heart.*

From the pots and pans in Grandma's kitchen cabinets,

the dented coffee table,

the classroom desks,

the bongos in
the fall festival,

and each marching band,

the rhythm from Miles Giles' heart will continue to echo.

Pa pa pa pa,
Pa pa pa pa –
Pa pa pa
Pa pa pa –
Pa pa pa pa!